Publisher	**Peter Cannon**
Photographer	**Blue Max**
Art Director	**Charles Lyon**
Design	**Doug Behrens**
Print Consultants	**Richard W. Lyday Sr.**
	David Simonson

Peter Cannon extends a special thanks to Strapped Inc.

Blue Max would like to thank Pearl McFeeley,
Charles McFeeley, Laura and Carlton Holt, Kenneth Lange,
Windward Aviation, Brian Sweeney, Rob Kaplan,
Doug Hunt, FEMA and SBA.

Charlie and Leslie Lyon want to thank Paul and Dolores Lyon,
Lewis and Betty Lou Connell, Papa Wharton, Gary Propper,
Drew Kampion, Mark Summary and Bjorn Dunkerbeck.

Printed by Everbest Printing Co. LTD, Hong Kong.

Color Saperation by Ocean Graphic Co. LTD, Hong Kong.

First Printing 1997

10 9 8 7 6 5 4 3 2 1

ISBN 0-9658986-0-1

Library of Congress Catalog Card Number: 97-073481

JAWS
MAUI™

Photography by Blue Max

Written by Charlie and Leslie Lyon

We extend our appreciation to the following people for their adventurous spirits, their dedication and their generosity in sharing their experiences with us, without which the following images and story would not be possible.

Tiger Espere

Laird Hamilton

Dave Kalama

Mike Waltze

Darrick Doerner

Pete Cabrinha

Rush Randle

Brett Lickle

Mark Angulo

Buzzy Kerbox

Archie Kalepa

Brock Little

Wally Froiseth

Don Shear

Gerry Lopez

Dick Brewer

Jeff Timpone

Victor Lopez

Dave Nash

Lyon Hamilton

Brian Keaulana

Michel Larronde

Robby Naish

Mike Stewart

Jason Polakow

Alex Aguera

Sierra Emory

Robbie Seeger

Luke Hargreaves

Bjorn Dunkerbeck

Josh Stone

Paul Bryan

Anders Bringdal

Hidemi Furuya

Keith Taboul

Greg Aguera

Paul Miller

Bob Haskins

Larry Stanley

Mike (Thor) Horgan

Mahalo to Peter W. Cannon for bringing solidarity to this endeavor.

I'm just damn lucky that none of those guys threw me off the cliff during the three years I was photographing them. Thanks.

— Blue Max

We want to thank Patrick McFeeley for his confidence in us. It was a true pleasure to work with his incredible photography. Mahalo nui loa to Tiger Espere, who put us on the correct path for the project. Also, thanks to Beverly Johnsen who helped it all make sense. A special thanks to Barry Spanier for his counsel.

— Charlie and Leslie Lyon

Salt water mists sweep up the cliffs, filling the air. The ground trembles under foot as boulders rumble up the shore, tossed like pebbles by the pounding surf. Lines of water roll in from the northwest. Tiny dots carve white trails across the blue ocean. One at a time the open ocean swell reaches the shallow shelf and jumps up. A jet ski, with surfer in tow, matches the wave's speed and whips the surfer into the peak. The wave rider brings a sobering sense of scale to the breaking wave. Glancing back toward Haleakala, the lush valley at Pe'ahi traces the path cut by the water shaping the island for thousands of years. It is appropriate that this place we call Jaws be on the island of Maui who opens up only to those who take the time to watch and learn.

What makes a man put himself in such peril? As observers we can only speculate. Watermen live every moment of every day with a driving desire inside them. Do they crave adrenalin? Are they searching for glory and fame? We asked these questions of the men who pioneered tow-in surfing. What we found surprised us. These men hold a deep sense of commitment to each other, to the island and to the ocean that surrounds us. We realized they are not daredevils, but men who take calculated risks, having a solid understanding of their environment and their equipment. They are men with an inner quality that is strengthened with each ridden wave.

Our search for understanding led us to Pua Ka'ilima O Kawaihae on the Big Island of Hawai'i. We spoke with Tiger Espere, legendary Waterman, and asked him what big wave riders have in common that enables them to venture out into huge surf. Here are his na mana'o (thoughts).

· · · · · ·

For me, and I think I can speak for other surfers too, it would be the Freedom. When you're out surfing, only you can produce the energy you want to put into it. We start off with small waves and we produce that energy, but the energy keeps getting bigger and bigger until your waves get bigger and bigger. Finally when you're outside, sitting out there and the waves are thirty feet, you've worked your way up to that height, but not overnight. It takes years of experiencing and riding because you're searching at the height of yourself and the Freedom. Some find Freedom riding two foot waves and some experience Freedom on a thirty foot wave. To them, that's the height they want to reach.

Along those stages as you're getting bigger waves, a lot of ego comes into play. That is the thing you really fight within yourself. For me, it was a big ego thing. The first time paddling out at Sunset, I never rode that place before. What drove me out there? It was my ego that put me out there because it was the first time. But as you keep riding the place your Inner Self is telling you that this is not the way to do this.

Your Inner Self tells you that you're dealing with something that's not in your hands, and it's in the hands of the Creator. When you find that spot, that's when you really get to enjoy who you really are and the wave becomes a part of you. It's always become a part of me. When I paddle out there, I am the wave. The surfboard is me. I am part of the surfboard. We are all one. When you find that thing, you truly understand what Freedom is all about. It's got nothing to do with your hard times on land because that all disappears. All the bills you have to pay, that all disappears when you're out there. I think that's what surfers strive for, to forget about the things that hang on to them when they walk out of the water. When you get out there, it's like there's no law. You don't have to associate with anybody's hangups but your own. You go out there and you deal with it. You realize, boy, you're just a little nobody.

All the old surfers, like Kealoha Ka'io, Greg Knoll, Peter Cole, Fred Van Dyke, Jose Angel, Buzzy Trent, George Downing, Wally Froiseth, they were all the pioneers. I was very fortunate to be one of their students. They took care of me when I was outside there. They taught me the value of Life and how special it is. They were sharing and they showed me how to do it. They just brought me to another height, to another level in myself.

I look at this tow-in, it's like the first time paddling out to Waimea. Tow-in is just another level of surfing. I have great respect for these tow-in pioneers because they've brought surfing to another height. I could never imagine riding waves over 30 feet.

And they are. I'm singing their song, I sing their names. I tell all my friends because I know all those guys. I want to support them and give them all the praises, the prayers and the caring because it takes a special being to go out in places like that when it's so big. They're the Peter Coles and the Buzzy Trents, all those great surfers, Greg Knoll. It's their time now. It's their way of securing surfing that can be enjoyable for them, for generations to come. It is a special feeling. You'd die for it. A lot of our great surfers have died.

Surfing has given me the dignity, the love for people, the love for the aina (land) and the water, and the love of my Akua (God). This is what I want to share with the kids that are coming up. Because right now, there's really no focus for them. There's too many distractions in their lives. The only thing that I can try to focus on is keeping the Hawaiian culture alive so they have something to be proud of. Surfing is part of this culture. I teach them about the place. I teach them the chant of the place where we surf, and the chant for the wind. They need to know all that because it's a part of the culture of surfing. Mostly, I teach about Aloha because without that, it just doesn't work.

The surfing chant consists of calling the winds. The winds create the surf for you. The chanting of the place calls the surf to be created where you want it. Everything starts with the wind chant, that creates the wave. Then when the wave has been created, where do you want this wave to go? Back out to sea? So you call. Everything has to be in order. You can't start in the middle and hope the front is going to come. You start from the front and work all the way back down to where you want it to be. Most surfers don't use the chants anymore because we lost them. I feel you have to find the balance. Part of the balance is knowing your culture and being proud of it. That's the other half of the battle. It's not your fault if you trample into my heiau (sacred place) and you don't know about it. It's not your fault. It's my fault. I should tell you about it so that you have great respect for it.

I don't care where you are, wherever the surf spot is, there were other beings that used to be there before. You cannot just trample in and not ask permission. So I teach all the basic things about coming to a place, giving a pule (prayer), and asking to be there. Ask the ancestors of the place to help you, to teach you, about this one particular place that you enter. It sounds weird for some people, but for us that is the right way. It shows respect for the place. That's been passed on for generations in our culture.

It boils down to your Spiritual Self. Because if you don't have that, you're not going to create the things that you want happening in your life. And that's basic. It's your Self, it's your Spiritual Self and what you want to accomplish. But if you're giving and caring, your name and your song will be sung for generations to come. And that, to me, is the height of anybody's surfing career. That's how you want to leave the arena of surfing, with people singing your song. Right now, you can be known as this and that, but just for right now. If you are never going to go over that hump about your Self, then

there's another guy coming up. When you go down, you'll never be known anymore. It's as if they won't see you anymore. We've known many surfers where nobody's singing their song anymore. We also know a lot of surfers that have passed away or they're still surfing and we're still singing their songs. No matter where I'm at, I can go live up in the hills or in the mountains and decide never to come back to the ocean. But they're always going to know that I was from the ocean a long time. And that song they're still singing.

My life in surfing has taken me to so many heights. The height I'm at right now is truly understanding the spiritual height of surfing. People can tell you a lot of things, but you have to experience it yourself. You have to find that certain energy inside so that you can become whole and you can truly be free. But it all comes with age and time. When you find that, you feel really settled. Everybody will get there in time, but they have to work on it. I've had my share of big waves and I'm very happy. I'm content. Even if I don't ever ride a wave over 6 feet, I know I did. It gave me that beautiful feeling and it's still inside me. We all have our own stories. We're all going to have our own feelings. That will never disappear.

• • • • • •

Let this book help you understand the Spirit that leads these men to challenge the place called Jaws. The action photography records their skill and courage. The scenic photography shares their environment. Let their words give you insight. Together, we will sing their songs into the twenty-first century.

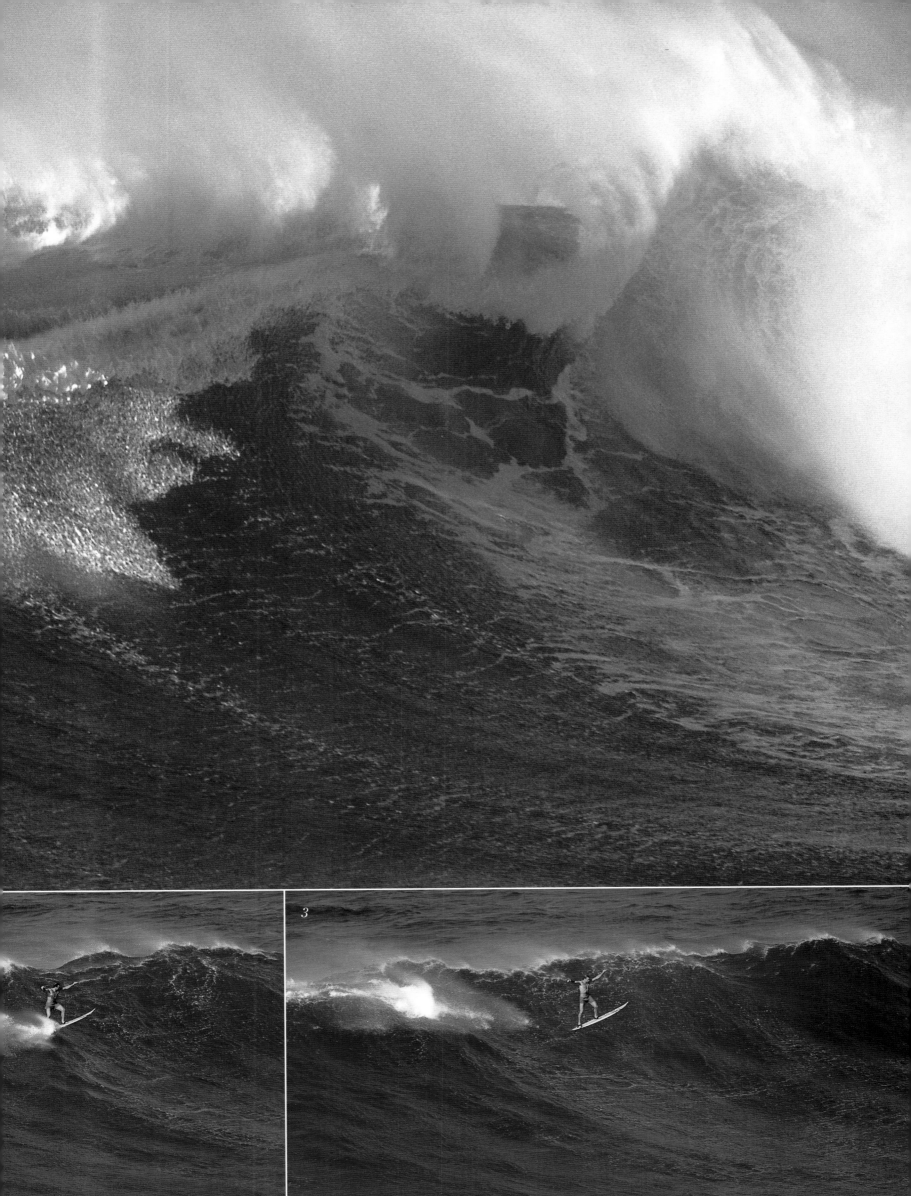

3

Laird Hamilton 7

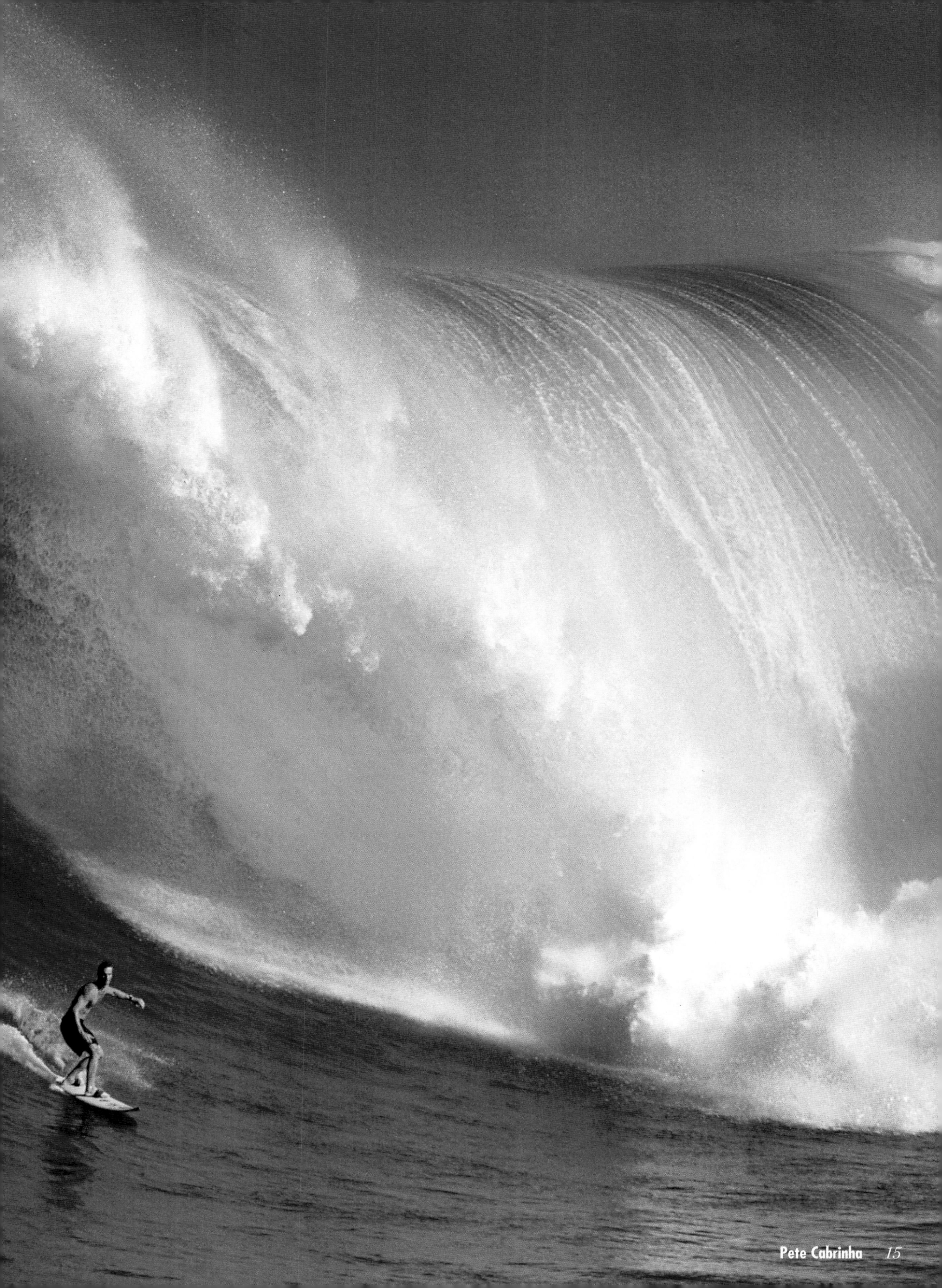

Pete Cabrinha

For many years, men came to watch and dream. They sat on the cliffs, meditating on the perfect wave, plotting and scheming about the time when they could try their best to ride it. There were seemingly insurmountable obstacles; the Volkswagen-sized boulders rolling around in the shore break, the sheer mass of the waves, the isolation. But as with watermen of the past, these men knew that through their observations, their experiences and new technology, they could figure out how to have fun here, too.

Maui's rural setting lends itself to the more adventurous of spirits. There are many places, like Jaws, that are difficult to reach, but well worth the trouble of getting there. *"We used to do a lot of dirtbiking. You would get to places after a couple of hours riding that you couldn't reach in a day of walking and still get back before dark. We would just be in these places and think, 'Wow, I wonder how many people have actually stood right here?' We're not through exploring."* – Mike Waltze

There are twenty ways to turn each morning for people who enjoy Maui and the surrounding ocean. The weather conditions help them decide which activity would be best. From which direction is the swell coming? Is the wind direction Kona or Trades and how strong are they blowing? Is it better to go surfing, paddleboarding, sailing or diving? Or should we go up the side of Haleakala and bomb down on mountain boards? *"Watermen live their lives in the ocean, learning about it and understanding all the cycles; the rhythms of the ocean, the rhythm of the swell, the rhythm of the sets."* – Mike Stewart

The ocean has always drawn people who are looking for adventure. It has a way of pulling at a person's soul and saying, "Come on. Forget about your chores. There's something better waiting for you out here." It's a bit different for everybody. Each person has their own threshold for excitement, and the men who surf Jaws seem to need more than most. They spend their time searching for ways to satisfy this need. Weather conditions do not allow them to surf or sail everyday, but they stay active, honing their skills and keeping their bodies, minds and spirits fit. When they call for the buoy reports that give them the swell size and intervals, they are ready for whatever comes. *"Imagine megatons of ocean and whitewater pounding and squeezing the life out of you, pushing your body down to depths you've never been before and contorting your body in ways it's never been. We stay in the ocean eight to ten hours a day. It builds endurance."* – Brian Keaulana

It is an interesting lifestyle, one that would be difficult for many people. In order to be able to take advantage of the weather conditions at a moment's notice, these men can't have regular, 9 to 5 jobs. They have to take things one day at a time. There's little chance to plan too far into the future. *"We didn't do this for press and money. We just did it because it was there. It was a challenge and no one else was doing it. Money and press came, but it was all after the fact. We do it for the love of it and we do it for each other, to keep each other alive and to help each other realize our dreams. Movies, magazines, books, the money; none of that stuff is going to make a difference when you're stuck under a twenty foot wave. You're going to have flashes about your family, friends, everybody you love. None of that other stuff means anything."* – Mark Angulo

Since they are some of the best athletes in the world, they have product endorsements which pay the bills. If a sponsor wants them in Bali tomorrow, for the next three weeks, they go in an instant. But they always end up back on Maui, where the conditions are favorable for maintaining their lifestyle.

With all this excitement, it would seem these men would be impervious to things that would make another person edgy. But there is one thing that rattles them at night and robs them of sleep; knowing that a swell of significant size is on the way. *"There is so much noise from the wave itself. You can even hear it up at my house. That's the hardest part, hearing it all night the night before. I always tell myself I'm not going. That's the only way I can get to sleep."* – Brett Lickle

"*When that swell direction comes in, it swings around the tip of West Maui. The whole brunt force of that swell swings down the coast focused on the corner of Jaws. It comes in there and it's got 5 to 10 times the intensity that any other spot on that whole coast of Maui even gets from that swell.*" – Gerry Lopez

"The whole experience lasts twenty four hours. Because we live on Maui, Buoy-One is about twelve hours away, so we hear the report the day before. You immediately start getting your act together, checking out your ski and other equipment. All that preparation the day before gets you psyched up to do it. That night, I barely sleep. I get up at four or five o'clock, make some coffee and go check it in the dark. It's hard to see, but you can hear it. By the time I get to Maliko, I've had so much time preparing, I'm already psyched to do it. I just want it, want it bad. Then when it's all over, I'm still buzzing for another twelve hours. The memories last a lifetime."

– Pete Cabrinha

"When you're skiing, you know the bumps. They're there and they aren't going to move. This is a live mogul field where bumps just pop up randomly at any second. You need to be prepared to deal with that, especially as it gets a lot bigger and the waves start moving a lot quicker. Then, it's a whole other realm. It's like downhill. It's easier to connect the dots than follow the contour. Sometimes you do it on purpose, sometimes you don't. Sometimes you just do it out of survival." – Laird Hamilton

Laird Hamilton 33

"Tow-in surfing has changed the future of big wave surfing. Now, it's not just riding twenty foot waves and surviving. It's riding twenty foot waves and ripping them; tube rides, off the tops and cutbacks. This is stuff that nobody ever thought would be possible." – Buzzy Kerbox

"Everybody's partners. We watch each other so if somebody doesn't come up, you drop the guy you're towing and your rope in the channel and you head in. Sometimes you only have one chance at the guy that's down before the next wave. If you don't get him, you have to circle around. It's better to have another ski there so you can track each other on the way in. In between waves, the other guy on the ski is watching the guy that's down from the channel and pointing to where he's going." – Rush Randle

"Some days, it can be sunny and glassy with all your friends out. The mood is relaxed and you almost get giggly. But as soon as something goes wrong, then the whole mood immediately changes. If somebody gets in a bad situation, it turns into your worst nightmare. It sobers everybody up and then we remember what we're dealing with out here. Depending on the conditions, Jaws takes on a mood of it's own." – Pete Cabrinha

The Hawaiian Islands are unique. Plants, animals and people have evolved here as they have no where else on earth. The environment continues shaping its inhabitants, even as people keep trying to shape the environment. But anyone who has been here knows that

there are spirits and an energy that cannot be denied, that needs to be taken care of and respected. *"That place, from the bay (Pe'ahi) all the way up to the mountain, has a lot of energy. You feel it, if you walk up the valley. There are a lot of taro terraces and ancient hula stages. It's heavy up there."* – Archie Kalepa

Kūloa Point • Oheʻo Gulch

Waiʻanapanapa • Paʻiloa Bay

Ke'anae Peninsula

Part of the training needed for riding a place like Jaws is intellectual. Studying the ocean, the sky, the constantly changing conditions of nature brings an understanding that goes deeper. The observer relies on feelings, on flowing with the energy of a place, as much as knowing what the ocean is most likely to do. *"You've got to listen to that voice. It's like if I was going windsurfing and went into the back of the truck. I started pulling out the universal and it got caught on something. Then, I started pulling out the booms and they got caught. If everything starts getting caught on everything, throw it back in the truck and go do something else. Today's not the kind of day to go windsurfing."* – Brett Lickle

"These days were so clean and readable, it became more of a playful thing. We were able to get a little more aggressive riding them. I had a tremendous amount of fun that day." – Dave Kalama

"*I showed up at Maliko and Darrick had just come in. His veins were popping out of his neck while explaining how gnarly it was. Darrick charges, so I had a real indicator of what I was about to do, so I was real cautious.*" – Mike Stewart

"I think it's an honor that we have the opportunity to share with people like Brian and Archie the things that we're doing. The greatest thing about this is that it's a team thing. Hawaiian is in your heart and in your spirit, you know, not in the color of your skin." — Laird Hamilton

"We'd seen the pictures of Jaws and heard about it. Then one day, Darrick and Laird called us. They said, 'It's happening! You guys want to come over? Drop everything. Don't bring any-thing. Just hop on over.' So, we went. Mike, Brock and I drove straight to the cliff from the airport. We must have been between sets because it didn't look like the pictures. We went down and met up with all the guys and made it out to Jaws. Then Mike, Brock and I caught our first waves. And Mike's face, his smile was so big and wide. He looked like one little kid. We were just flipping out. The place was just such perfection." – Brian Keaulana

"It all just gets so cartoonish and unreal. You are out there passing up eighteen footers to catch more twenty footers. The thrill of catching that big of a wave, you can't compare it to anything." – Pete Cabrinha

The Hawaiian Islands are constantly changing, growing and eroding in a give and take with natural forces. Today's watermen also adapt to the times, taking lessons from the past and carving them to fit the present. One example of this is the voyaging canoe Hawai'iloa.

"I sailed Hawai'iloa back from Nuku Hiva. The canoe taught me how to take care of people and how to take care of the canoe, most of all. We learned to make smart decisions for safety, not just for ourselves, but for the canoe first. When you come into port, you don't just dive off and forget about that canoe, leaving it dirty and all. That canoe took care of you. If you aren't going to take care of the canoe, something's going to happen. On Hawai'iloa, the canoe itself is living. I think of the canoe like it is the Earth. That's your land right there. You've got to take care of that piece of land you are on until you cross over. You can have all the knowledge in the world, but that's one spiritual trip, brah. If you don't respect that, you lose the feeling.

The sailing canoe Hawai'iloa was built out of traditional materials and it proved itself as a sea worthy voyaging canoe. These two tasks further proved that the ancient Hawaiians were the world's best watermen. Wally Froiseth, one of the fathers of big wave surfing, was also the overseer of the Hawai'iloa's construction. He crewed with us on the voyage. He is in his seventies. He had more energy than anybody else on the canoe. When there was a task at hand, he was the first one up to do it. As a waterman, you want to share that experience. The best way for you to teach is by doing. When they see how you commit yourself to the environment then the people maybe learn from that and it will rub off on them." – Archie Kalepa

The same spirit that inspired Wally Froiseth to pioneer big wave surfing as a young man, has been passed down to the young pioneers of today. These men use the same energy in many facets of their lives, inspiring the big wave riders of tomorrow.

"You're out there with a bunch of guys who you know would come after you in a bad situation. So, you're putting a lot of trust in them and they're putting a lot of trust in you. That in itself is pretty inspiring. I look at the power of Dave's and Laird's surfing for inspiration. I look at Rush Randle for the aerial aspect of surfing." – Pete Cabrinha

"One thing that's so insane about riding Jaws is that after growing up all those years with the cartoons in the surf mags, like Antman and Wilbur Kookmeyer, these characters on these huge waves, I always looked at them and thought, 'That's just impossible. You could never do that.' Now I look at these photos of my friends on these waves and I think, 'Oh my God. I remember that Wilbur Kookmeyer episode when I was nine. Wow, this is real and this is my friend. Look at this thing!'" – Rush Randle

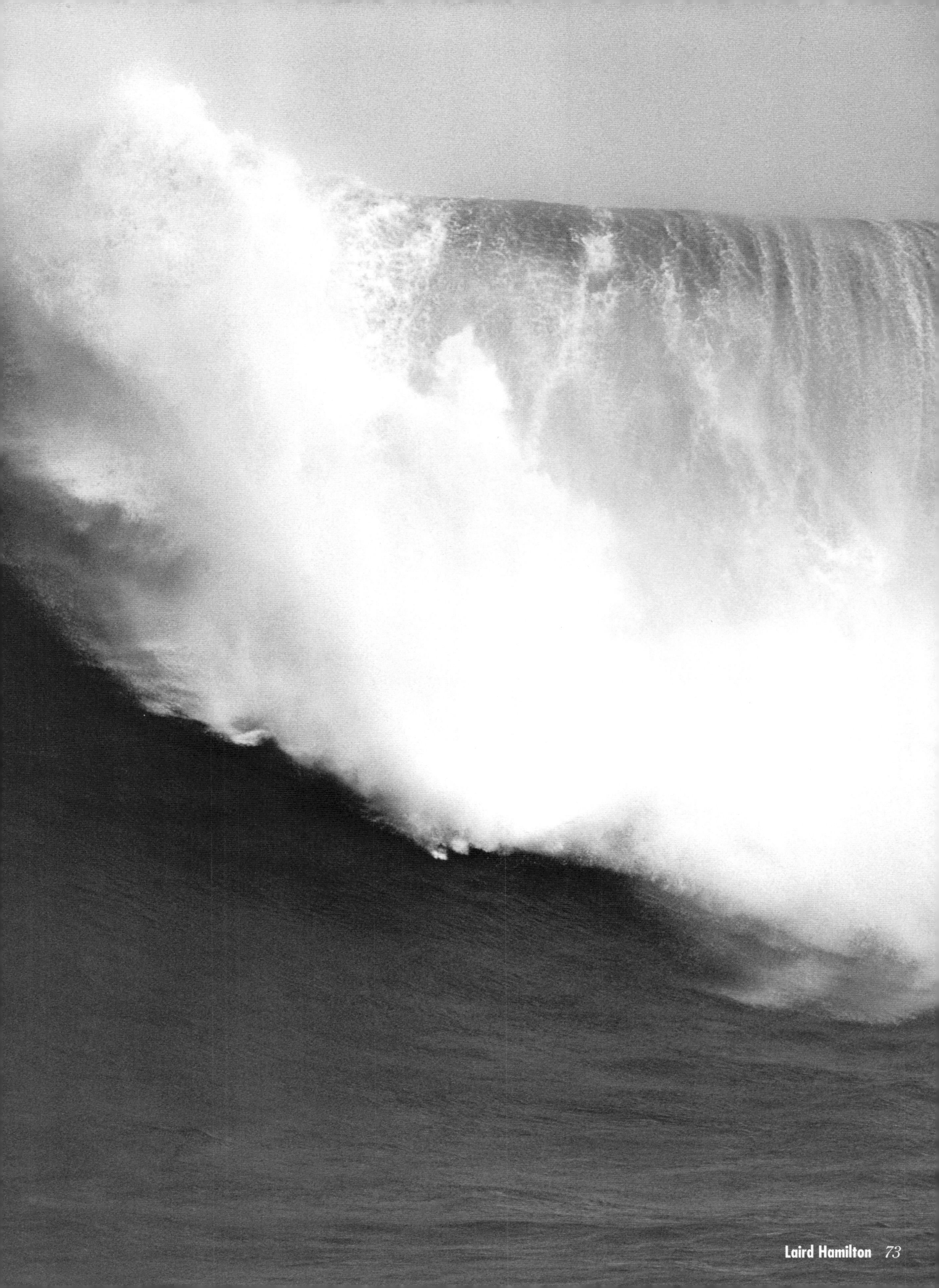

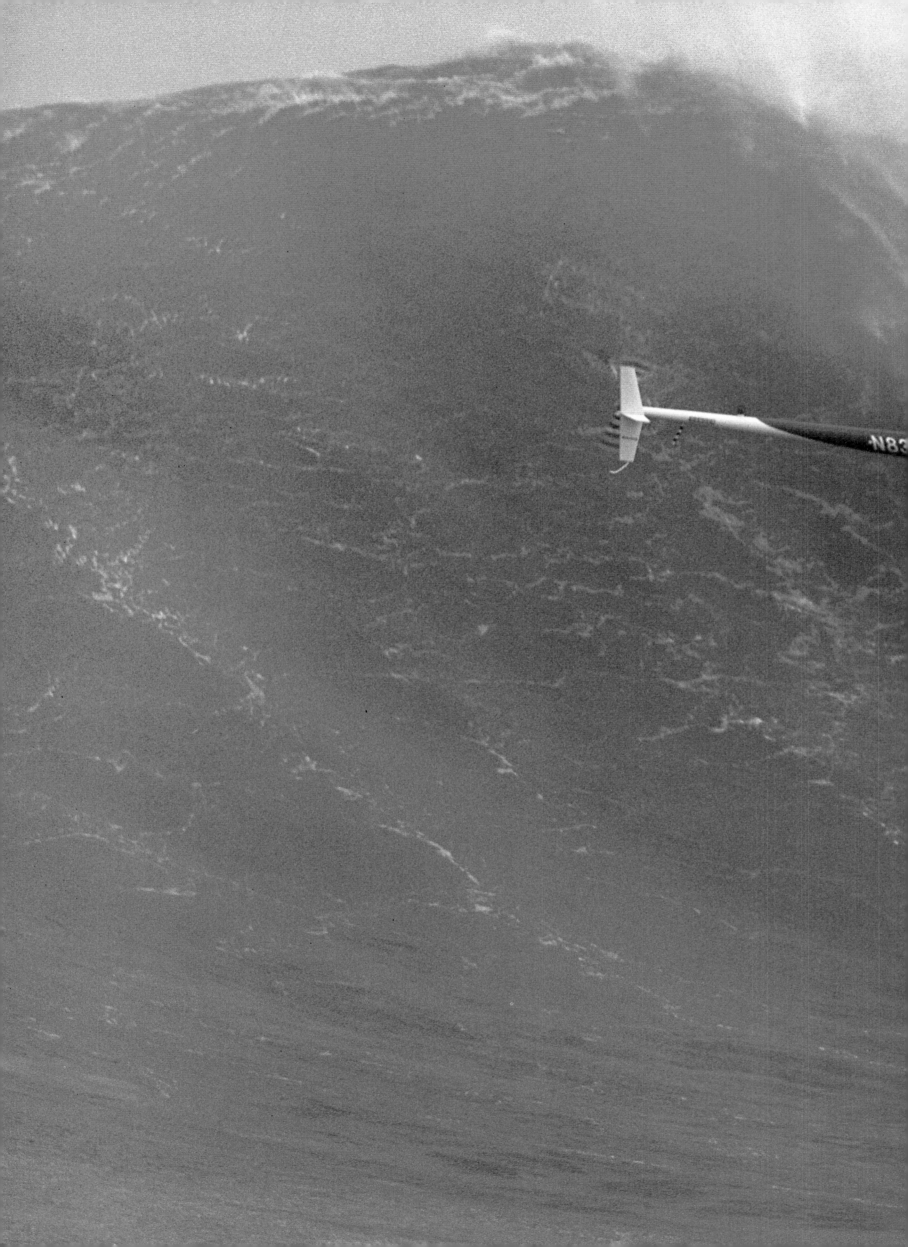

"There are big waves I do remember, but most of the time you're in a mind space. You're in the zone with that wave; that split second, that chop in front of you, the way the wave is setting up down the line. You're not really concentrating on what's behind you or even thinking about it. It's strange because at that moment you're focused on the two inches in front of your board and fifty to a hundred feet down the line in a tunnel vision. It's like looking through the lens of a camera where everything is all out of focus except that little dot in the middle. Everything is just slow motion." – Rush Randle

"I've seen Laird get barrelled. I've seen Dave get barrelled. I've seen Pete get barrelled. I've seen Mike get barrelled. I've seen Darrick get barrelled and Rush get barrelled. I think I'm the only one that never got barrelled out there. I hope to stay that way a long time because these guys are crazy, brah." – Mark Angulo

"I got a call from one of those daytime talk shows. They were doing a show on daredevils. They said they'd like to get me on the show and wanted to know more about what we did, so I told them to get their hands on the video, 'Wake Up Call'. A few days later, the producer called me back and said, 'Gosh, I can really appreciate what you guys are doing because I've surfed big waves before. But we can't have this segment on our show because it just doesn't look dangerous enough on film. You guys make it look too easy. Honestly, the general public won't really see it as dangerous. You guys are making every wave. We want to see someone go over the falls. We want a body count!'" – Pete Cabrinha

Riding waves at Jaws is not like wave riding anywhere else. If a person decides to participate, they have to be willing to play a role in a life threatening scenario. A split second decision could make the difference between saving a fallen rider or not.

"These guys always do something. There's not even a thought in their minds. They're beyond the think stage. They're already reacting. They know what has to be done and how they're going to save somebody." – Victor Lopez

Halea Kala 93

"Fear, in a physical sense, to me means tightening your muscles in preparing yourself for impact or fighting. I still have fear obviously, because I have a fear of dying, but I'm trying not to let the fear have control over my body. Usually, when you experience fear is when you need to be as loose as you can possibly be and focused on the task rather than tightening up. Your movement needs to be as agile and spontaneous as it possibly can be. Fear just exists. That's the way it is. The better you can deal with it the more prepared you are for any situation." – Dave Kalama

Pete Cabrinha

"*I remember the last time I used a leash. I got caught inside, down at the end. Although it wasn't a giant wave, it was still a wave I didn't want to deal with too much. It broke right in front of me. I swam down, keeping my eyes open. I was staying in clear water, so when I was pulling, I was pulling pretty good. I could see the boils right behind me. Then, all of a sudden, the board started to pull and I started to go backwards towards the boils. I said to myself, 'No way! I'm not going into those things!' They were just dropping straight down in big columns. So, I started pulling extra hard with my arms. Then, luckily, the leash snapped so I was able to swim away from them and get back up. After that, it was no more leashes for me.*" — Dave Kalama

2

"That tube I got was on a smaller west bowl. I saw the curtain and just pulled in. When I saw that opening, I said, 'I'm going out that opening.' I made it out and it was a great feeling. Usually, you come out and you're all hooting and hollering, but this was more like coming back from an out of body experience; just overwhelmed." – Dave Kalama

"*If the lip hit me, I think it would dismember me. You would have to be someone like Laird to take a hit like that.*" – Gerry Lopez

"At that moment of release from the tow rope, you get freed. The situation requires your full focus and concentration. I've had the blessing to be in that situation many times in my life. It becomes a very comfortable place to be. You've been there. It's familiar and you know it." – Laird Hamilton

"The safety of the channel is more a state of mind than a real place because you can see it. The guys are sitting on the jet ski. They're only fifty feet away. It seems that you could almost dive that far." – Gerry Lopez

"I ended up behind Laird on a wave and I could have followed him, but that left was just beckoning. I took a chance. You can go left pretty safely up to about fifteen feet. If it gets any bigger, the left takes you directly into a rock outcropping. I was hoping I could get out of it before it got to the rocks. I did and it was an insane ride." – Pete Cabrinha

"I never feel like I conquered it. I just feel lucky enough to ride a few big ones and get back in okay." – Pete Cabrinha

The idea of getting propelled into a wave is not a new concept. The ancient Hawaiians called it lele wa'a (canoe leaping). Seven men would take out a big canoe. Six paddlers would get up enough speed to catch a ground swell. The seventh man, holding his surfboard, would leap off the boat onto the wave and ride it. Today's tow-in surfing has taken old ideas and applied new technology for a modern twist.

There's a relatively short history to tow-in surfing itself, but it definitely has its roots in other board-riding sports, especially windsurfing. The first successful sessions on larger waves at Jaws were on sailboards. Many of these watermen still enjoy sailing there. These men combined their ocean experiences in developing this new facet of surfing. In their pursuit of big waves, Laird Hamilton, Buzzy Kerbox and Darrick Doerner started taking a Zodiac to the outer reefs on O'ahu's north shore and towing each other into waves. They were riding their traditional big wave guns originally designed for paddling into waves.

Meanwhile on Maui, a handful of guys, Mark Angulo, Mike Watlze, Rush Randle, Pete Cabrinha, Brett Lickle and Dave Kalama, put footstraps on their short surfboards so that they could experience the same level of performance to which they were accustomed while windsurfing. Seeing what they were doing strapped to short boards, Laird had Dick Brewer shape him a scaled down gun with foot straps for his towing excursions. From this Laird, Buzzy and Darrick realized they could ride the same large surf on smaller boards as long as they had footstraps. At the speeds they were reaching, their feet had to be strapped on so that when they hit the bumps, the board would come up with them, and stay with them. The straps kept them from flying off. The Zodiac was tossed aside for the more efficient and maneuverable jet ski, and

modern tow-in was born. They brought the new sport to Maui. The two groups joined up and the equipment evolved with each session at Jaws. For a more in-depth history of tow-in surfing, read *JATO: Jet Assisted Take-Off* written by Gerry Lopez in The Surfer's Journal Vol. 4, No. 1, Spring 1995.

Usually, a surfboard design was a giant compromise. It had to be big enough to paddle, but small enough to turn; have thick enough rails so it didn't get buried in the flats, but not so thick that you couldn't sink it. When they did not have to factor in paddling, suddenly the performance aspect widened. ***"Paddling? These guys don't even get their hair wet."*** – Gerry Lopez

For big wave surfboard design, all the rules were not only broken, they were reversed. Every square inch of surface area that water touched was friction. The more surface area, the more friction. The smaller boards were reaching high speeds, but they wouldn't go any faster. They took away more foam and the boards became lighter, but harder to control at the higher speeds. All of a sudden, the boards wanted to fly. With that much board out of the water, they were no longer dealing with only hydrodynamics. They had to factor in aerodynamics as well. They started weighting their boards with lead plates and routing grooves and filling them with BBs. ***"In tow surfing, getting a lot of air is a fact of life. You get wind lifting the nose of your board, so you end up doing a lot of tail landings. So we added lead weights to our boards. I carry mine just in front of my front foot. It makes it fly truer. Once it takes off, you have more control. It wants to fly like a dart. It really is fun. You scare yourself to death, then you come in laughing."*** – Pete Cabrinha

"We were just windsurfers when we hooked up with Jeff. He was into it because he was a surfer and a shaper for so long. He had all the modern technology and the talent to build them. We just kept getting boards and changing them and getting more. By the time Laird came back with the towing idea, we were already tuned into strap boards." – Rush Randle

The best shapers were the ones able to keep an open mind. Gerry Lopez and Jeff Timpone were on Maui keeping up with the changing needs of the tow-in surfers. Gerry's boards were the first good interpretations of Brewer's tow-boards. Then Jeff started to make his interpretation of the Brewer boards. Soon after, he went in his own direction, working closely with Dave Kalama, Rush Randle, Brett Lickle and Pete Cabrinha, developing their own concepts of rocker lines, outlines and fin configurations. *"Watching them live and on film, I get a feel for what needs to be changed and how the board goes through the water. I can see from one board to the next which one is going faster, which one's releasing easier."* – Jeff Timpone

Through all their experiments, they came back full circle to more traditional materials. More weight was better, so they began making wood blanks instead of using foam. The progress in Jeff's designs enabled the riders to make big progress in their techniques. There was no "One Board Fits All" design. The boards were all custom-made, the design changing with each person. The placement of the footstraps, the weight of the rider, the increased speed of the jet ski, all these factors made each board unique.

"You have to have the utmost confidence in your board when you're surfing waves that big. The board can't even be a doubt in your mind. Whatever the design is, as long as you are completely confident in the equipment, then you're going to surf better because of it. You've got to be somewhat aggressive just to keep everything together because the wave is trying to tear you apart." – Dave Kalama

"It gives me a sense of accomplishment. As a shaper, it makes you realize that you're doing something right. It's not just building a board, it's life and death out there. When it gets big, it's the real thing and I can see how the boards are a major part of that. It's not so much the equipment as the guy. You've got to feel comfortable and confident in the board, but so much of it is the guy standing on top of it." – Jeff Timpone

Board design wasn't the only change being made. By using the jet ski to tow each other into the waves, the whole experience in the water had to be tuned up. The sport evolved from an individual event to a team effort. *"What's the funnest thing about Christmas, getting the presents or knowing you got this cool present for your mom or dad and you can't wait for them to open it? Towing your friend into a wave is the same thing. When he comes out hooting and hollering, you know that you participated in that wave, too. You're the one that got him in, so it's different than normal surfing or sailing. It's a team experience."* – Mark Angulo

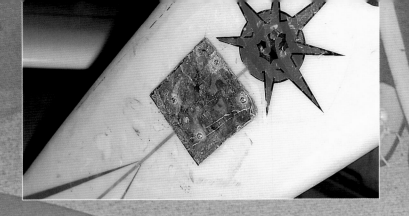

A good driver was key. He could place the rider in the best or worst possible place. Windsurfing experience made them better drivers because they were familiar with standing on top of swells two hundred yards out and selecting waves. *"When you're towing around out there and picking a wave, they're all about the same height, but they are different colors. The bigger ones are deeper and darker, meaner and more ominous looking. There are normally a couple of smaller ones before and after the big ones. Sometimes the big one is the one behind the one that looks big. It's the one with all the power and it also has that wave in front to clean up anything like chop and bumps."* – Rush Randle

Communication between the driver and the rider became essential. *"That's where the practice comes in. We have a full hand signal set up that we work with: faster, slower, left, right, first wave, second wave. We're always communicating."* – Brett Lickle

The jet ski enabled them to surf in spots that were previously inaccessible. They had been checking the waves at Jaws for years, eyeing the perfect waves, watching the boulders pummel the shore. They had even braved the steep cliff and paddled out on traditional big wave equipment with little success. They had enjoyed windsurfing it, but were at the mercy of the wind to power them into the wave. Now they could launch from a protected bay several miles away.

They had the technology to surf gargantuan waves and be safer and have more fun. *"A big wave that shifts is dangerous. But a big wave that shifts on a jet ski is a playground."* – Brett Lickle

Safety is always of primary concern. Part of the equipment they have adapted is the rescue sled developed by the Hawaiian Water Patrol. It looks like a giant body board with handles down both sides. This sled is attached to the rear of the ski, enabling the driver to make a more efficient rescue without coming to a stop. Usually there is somebody on a ski patrolling the inside, watching from the channel and riding safety. If somebody goes down, he's the first person to know. He can signal the others and get in and out of the impact zone faster. Everyone is watching out for each other. *"You just turn your back on that next wave and you're just waiting for that head to pop up. You know that wave's behind you. It doesn't matter. You've got no choice. Your friend's down thirty feet. You've got to at least be there to give him the chance to not take another one on the head. Anytime I've been in the water and someone's come and grabbed me has been a big eye popper. While they're coming in, they're not looking at the wave. They're just looking at you. You're looking out and all you see is that big giant mammoth piece of water coming at you. You're going, 'Oh my God! I hope my hand doesn't slip.'"* – Mark Angulo

In this kind of surf, they needed to partner-up. By discussing the worst possible situations, they are prepared before they head out. The rescue techniques have to be practiced. The driver needs to have an arsenal of options. He makes a split-second decision based on the particular situation, and they might only have one shot. The correct response is the one that gets the guy out alive. *"Brian Keaulana said, 'We're not risk takers. We are risk technicians.' Brian is definitely a risk technician. He really picks apart a*

Even with all the planning and experience, they never know when something could go wrong. *"Something did happen on Thanksgiving Day that I still get all sweaty palmed about. It was at the end of the session. I was sitting outside on my board, resting. Mike was driving me, so he was sitting on the ski right next to me. I looked down and my footstrap was completely off. One side was just flopping in the water. The wave just before, I had this late drop with a bunch of bumps at the top of the wave. As I launched over the ledge, I caught lots of air. If my strap came undone then, I'd probably be history now. It was the biggest, fattest wave I have ever had."* – Pete Cabrinha

"My most frightening experience out there was on a pretty good sized wave. I remember going over a chop and spinning out just enough to catch my inside rail. Then I just huli'd (turned) head over heels two or three times down the face of the wave. I ripped my wetsuit from the middle in the front above my waistline down through the crotch up to my zipper in the back just from hitting the water so hard. I also had mild whiplash, front and back. Anyway, I penetrated and came out the back. As soon as I grabbed my board, I looked up and saw the biggest thing I'd ever seen before. I knew if I didn't get through this wave I was going to die. This wave looked like a tsunami, just a huge wall of water. I thought, 'This is nuts. I'm out of here. This is not real.' I remember paddling as hard as I could straight at it, then dunking down. I was pointing the board straight down, standing on the tail to get as deep as I could go. Then I was kicking my legs as hard as I could. I remember coming up behind the wave and seeing Pete coming at me on a ski, but the wave behind him was just as big, if not bigger than the one I was laying on. Pete had a split second to get me. I was on top of this barrel, so big it was like Niagara Falls. I was just paddling so hard looking at Pete, and Pete's face said, 'If he goes back over, he's dust.' I started to feel it pulling me backwards. I held on just long enough for Pete to reach me as whitewater was shooting up. I grabbed the side of the sled and we gunned it out of there. My leash luckily snapped because it was like an anchor. We just cleared the next wave. Any further in or out, I wouldn't have made it." – Rush Randle

situation very quickly, beginning with the worst case scenario and working backwards from there. If you look at our operation; the skis, all the safety equipment, the sleds and our technique, you might even say we are risk technicians."* – Pete Cabrinha

They know that in order to survive the extreme conditions at Jaws, they need to be prepared mentally and physically. They are water safety certified and continue to sharpen their skills. This, combined with a vast experience in varied conditions, makes them better prepared in huge surf. They all believe they haven't even seen a big swell yet. They work as a team, but they're prepared to be out there on their own. They never know when a big set may come through and take out every boat and ski. *"Before you go out there, you have to sit down and study it. How many waves are in a set? How far apart are they breaking? What direction is it coming from? Are there swings in the swell? Which way is the current moving, and how fast does it move? How much of an impact does that white water drive onto the bottom of the ocean?"* – Brian Keaulana

"I was there on Thanksgiving and decided not to go out. I just didn't feel comfortable going out there that day. Everybody has got to know their limits. The one thing I remember about Lyon Hamilton's wave was that he was over towards the shoulder, but it was one of those macker end bowls that punish. He kind of slowed down with a little mini stall zigzag and then went straight down and came over a chop. Right before he dropped over it, he tried to set his rail, but when he came over, his board went straight for a split second. It didn't even turn. He went straight down on his side, which was actually pretty good because he penetrated just enough so that he didn't get caught up on the top of the moving swell. He just went through the back. His board went so freakin' high. It was like a pinwheel. You're laying there just hoping that the semi goes right over you and you don't get caught in the drivetrain!" – Rush Randle

"When we pulled up, there was a set breaking a quarter to a half mile out from the usual lineup. It broke so far outside the regular lineup, I couldn't believe it. It was chilling. Laird was getting towed around by the helicopter. Kalama came up to us in the channel and said that their jet ski wasn't running very well. After seeing that set, we said, 'Hey, just take ours.' Laird caught some good ones. Kalama got some. Cabrinha got a few good ones and almost got bucked off. I'm glad he made it, because I wouldn't have wanted to see it if he didn't. Then Lyon went out, got one wave, went to the bottom and got bucked off. Luckily, he went through and came out the back. Then Lyon's board was just spinning in the lip of this twenty five foot wave. After that wipeout, we all packed it up and left. The whole thing was just chilling." – Gerry Lopez

If it goes up five feet in size, it goes up ten feet in thickness."
– Dave Kalama

"You see guys like Brock and Brian. It's almost like they want to get obliterated just to taste it."
– Mike Stewart

"Brock and I were on the same wave. I was in front, looking back at him. I didn't want him to get shut down back there, so I just rode way out in front and gave him all the room in the world. So Brock turns kind of close to the bottom and just fades into this pitted barrel. I see him as clear as day, just full round house around him, just swallowing and he's coming out. Just before he comes out, the lip crashes on top of his head and sucks his board over the top. Then, boom, he goes over. As he goes over, I kept surfing, cutting out. I was thinking, 'Okay. This is where he wiped out. This is where we're going to start to search and follow the current, because he could be straight down here to who knows where.' We see Brock's board bouncing around, but Brock is still under water. The second wave comes by and Brock still hasn't come up. All of a sudden, he pops up and I swear he was two hundred yards away from me. Waltze went in and grabbed him and, God, they went flying. These guys will lay their lives down and Waltze went right in." – Brian Keaulana

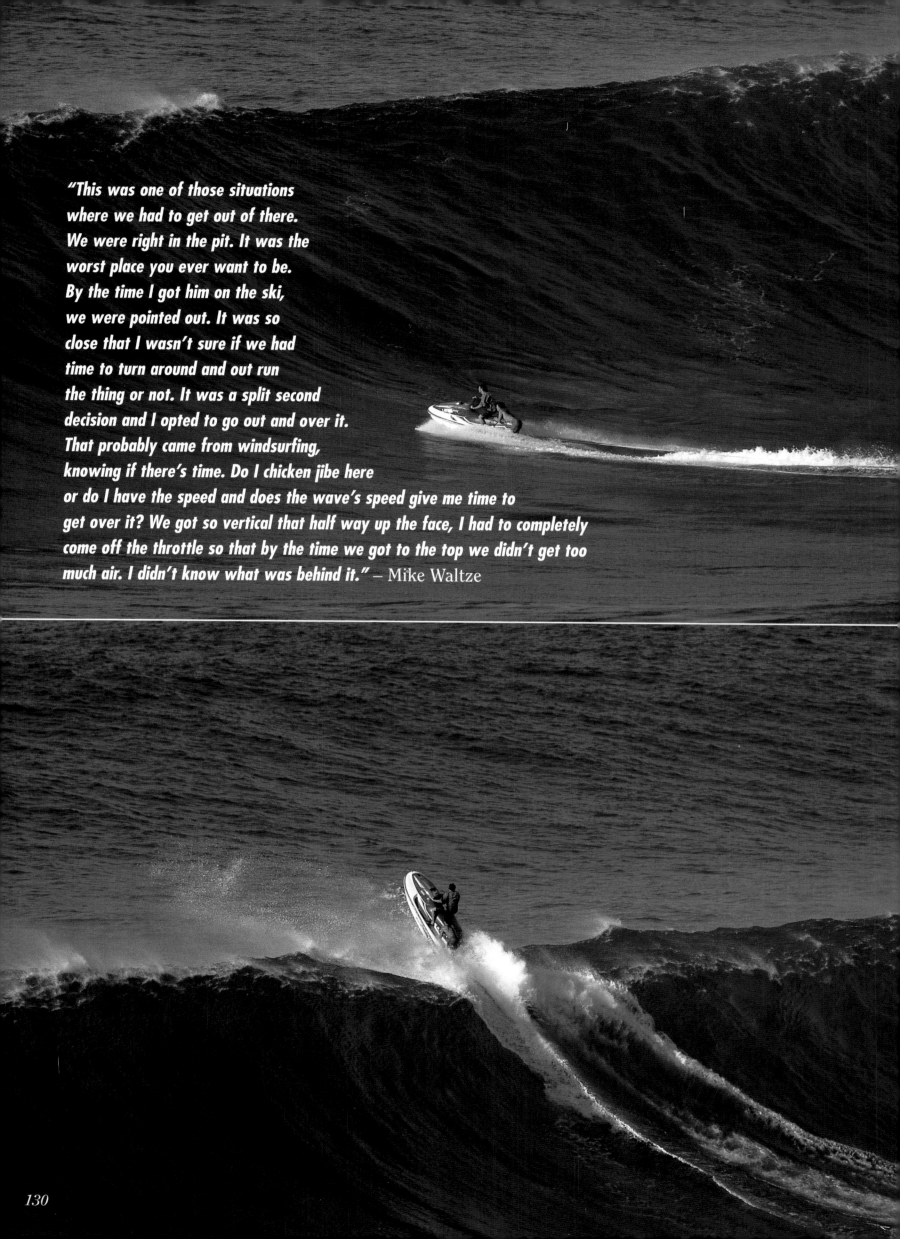

"This was one of those situations where we had to get out of there. We were right in the pit. It was the worst place you ever want to be. By the time I got him on the ski, we were pointed out. It was so close that I wasn't sure if we had time to turn around and out run the thing or not. It was a split second decision and I opted to go out and over it. That probably came from windsurfing, knowing if there's time. Do I chicken jibe here or do I have the speed and does the wave's speed give me time to get over it? We got so vertical that half way up the face, I had to completely come off the throttle so that by the time we got to the top we didn't get too much air. I didn't know what was behind it." — Mike Waltze

"On Thanksgiving Day, I got to surf the biggest waves I've ever ridden up until now. After that, I had a little different perspective on things, on the world in general. Things that I thought were so important, weren't as important as I thought they were. It was a kind of a reality check. I came out feeling stronger and everything got a lot more clear. All that stuff you fill your mind with, you realize that all of it is pretty insignificant." – Laird Hamilton

Dave Kalama

Rush Randle

"The people who really excel in this extreme sport are ocean people.
You cannot consider us to be surfers, windsurfers or bodyboarders.
That's just a part of who we are." – Brian Keaulana

"That release is incredible. I've heard it from everybody else. You can see the goosebumps on their bodies when they talk about it. My adrenalin comes up just from talking about it. There is no drug like it. There is nothing on earth that has done that to me."
– Michel Larronde

"I have had that feeling where that's it. That one moment you are riding the wave or jumping off that cliff is all that matters and your whole life is about that one particular moment. Everything's clear, everything just is and that's all that matters at that particular point. That's probably why big wave riders keep riding big waves. They get that feeling and once you experience it, you want to get back to it again. It's euphoric in a sense. Everybody in big waves and I'm sure in all other sports, we all want that same feeling. Actually, everybody in life, for that matter, wants to feel euphoric, no problems, enlightened, all of these things all at one moment where nothing matters except Being matters, you know? For me and my friends, and I'm sure big wave riders before and after me, that's our channel to that feeling."
– Dave Kalama

"My favorite is when it's fifteen, twenty feet and good. When it's over that size, survival instincts kick in." – Buzzy Kerbox

"Lokahi is mind, body and soul. To just strengthen your physical self is not enough. To strengthen yourself mentally is not enough. To strengthen yourself spiritually is not enough. To strengthen yourself physically, mentally and spiritually is Lokahi." – Brian Keaulana

"I've learned in the past that the mind is more powerful than the body. If the mind is a little off, then the body is a little off. But if the mind's on and the body's off, it'll go where the mind tells it to go and do what it tells it to do. Being in good physical shape will definitely increase your confidence which will increase your mind's power over your body." – Laird Hamilton

Laird Hamilton   *149*

"It's a totally active lifestyle. Can you imagine if you are getting that much adrenalin all the time? You can't just go into a cubicle and stare at the T.V." – Rush Randle

"Going out there with the strap guys was a very unique experience. They really treat each other like it's the last time they're going to see each other. Everybody cares about one another and looks after one another. This is actually bringing out a good side of surfing. It's different than when you go out paddle surfing where everybody is just thinking about catching their waves. They don't care about you." – Archie Kalepa

"Laird is the first wave man. He feels things out, then everybody takes his word for it. If Laird comes in and says, 'It's sh!@ty. Let's leave,' we leave. Nobody argues because if he doesn't want anything to do with it neither do you. You feel naked when Laird's not around, the group does. He sets the pace." – Brett Lickle

2

3

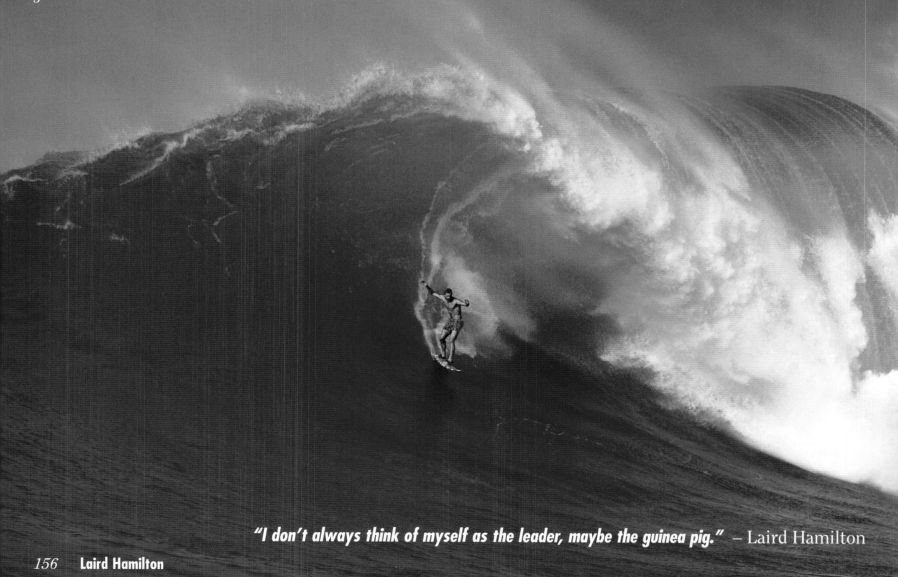

"I don't always think of myself as the leader, maybe the guinea pig." – Laird Hamilton

Dave Kalama

"As a surfer, Dave is right there with him. Dave is focused, but Laird is driven. He's doing it for a reason nobody else is doing it."
— Brett Lickle

Hana Coast

"That fresh water just gouged that channel out eighty to a hundred feet. That's why it's so ideal. The incredible thing is to have a wave that big with such a well defined channel. Every other big wave spot will close out. Like Waimea, it can close all the way across the bay."

Keopuku Rock   159

"There's no denying, Laird is the best big wave surfer in the world right now. No one can take that away from him, I don't think. Laird eggs you on to do stuff that you probably wouldn't have done. I don't think I would have gone out there and ridden some of those waves I did if it wasn't for Laird. He'll say, 'Let's go jump off this cliff.' You say, 'Yeah right.' But before you know it you're falling down in the air and landing in the water. He inspires people to do things they wouldn't do, but you get out there and you do it and you go, 'Wow! I could do it!' He shoulders some responsibility, too. He doesn't just take you out there, put you in a situation and not come get you. When the s#!t hits the fan, he's the first one to get concerned and get in there to settle the situation." – Mark Angulo

"Watermen use the ocean with all its mood swings for their enjoyment. That's the real watermen in my opinion." – Mike Waltze

Robby Naish *163*

1

"Mike's the best in the world. He's in a class of his own. He can do things that no one else in the world is going to be able to do and he's going to make them look easy." – Laird Hamilton

"It was surreal watching Mike Stewart out there. We design our boards seven feet long and extremely narrow so we can handle the speed, etc... Then here's Mike on a board that's a few feet long and it's wide and he's doing it. The wave looks so much bigger because he's laying down. It was impressive the way he attacked it with confidence, pulling in and making it. We do everything we can to avoid bad situations and he just pulls right in like it's nothing. This was cool for us because it gave us a different perspective. We didn't know if it was even possible. What kind of speed was he going to get or what would happen when he started going over the chop? Can you imagine the feeling laying prone on a twenty foot wave? I'd like to feel that." – Pete Cabrinha

"Jaws is a whole other level. Jaws is it. As far as I know, that's the heaviest wave I've surfed. This is another level that until recently was unknown. Just to ride it, just to see it top to bottom and spitting at twenty feet is something else. Jaws is a thick wave at twenty feet. I'm used to surfing thick waves at twelve feet, which are considered heavy waves by anyone in the surfing world. To go to Maui and do that is humbling."
– Mike Stewart

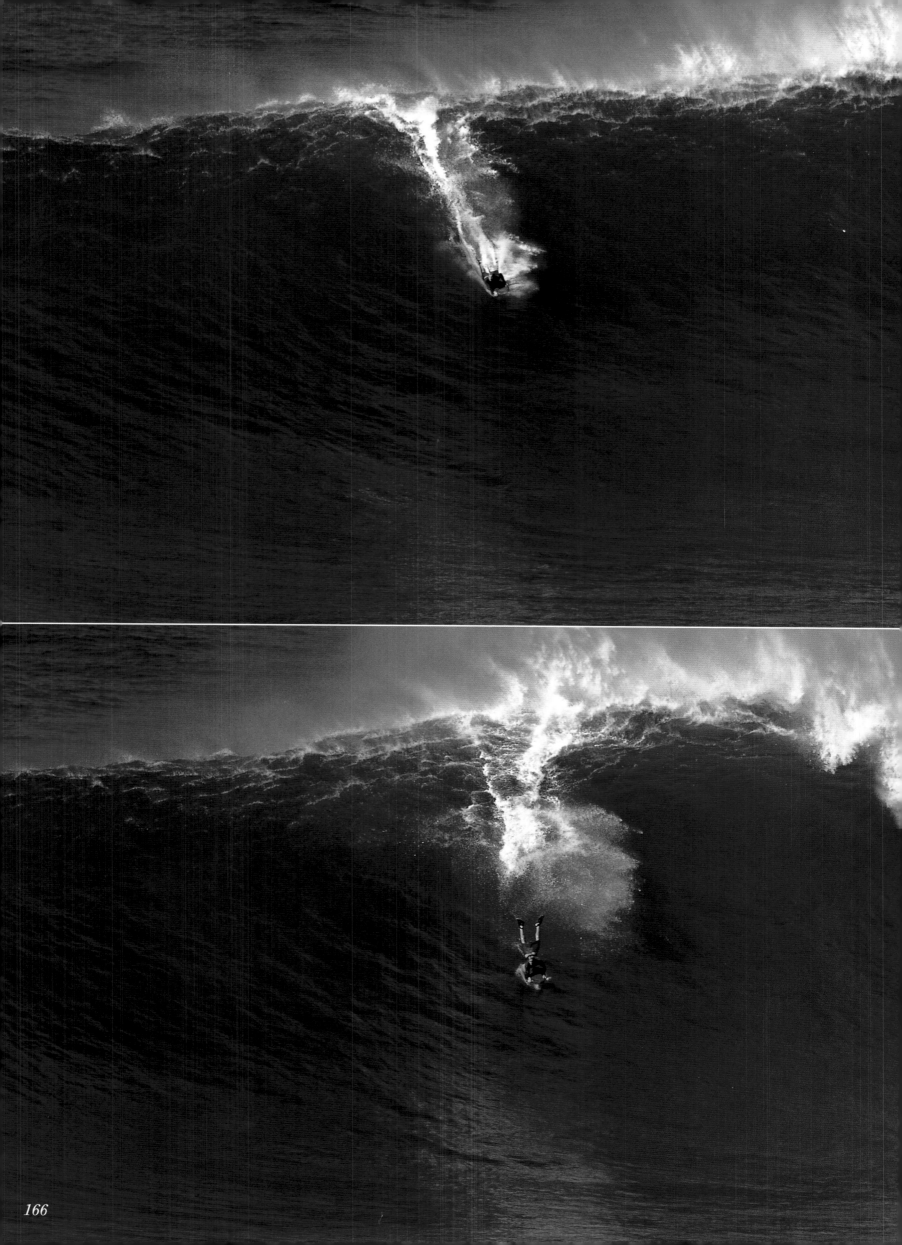

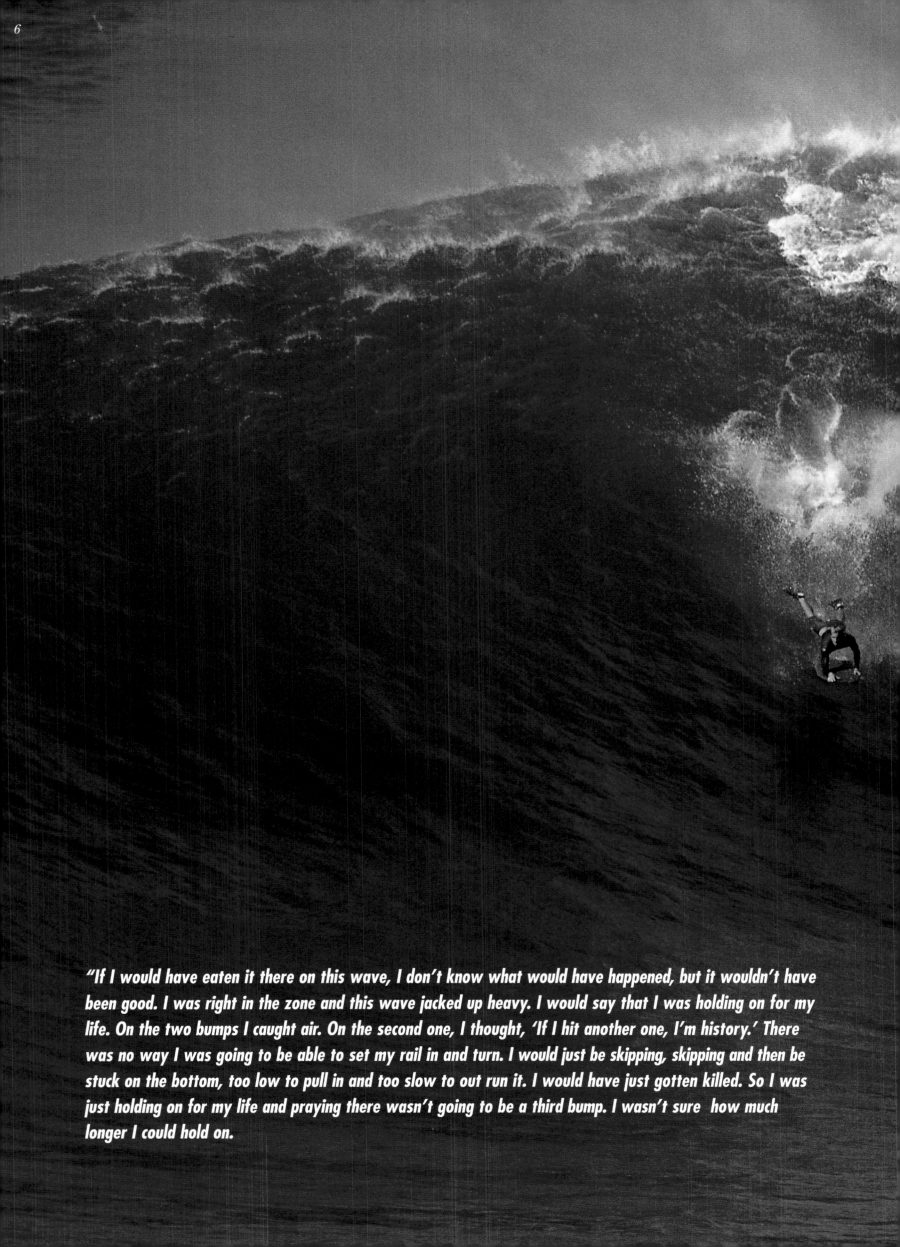

6

"If I would have eaten it there on this wave, I don't know what would have happened, but it wouldn't have been good. I was right in the zone and this wave jacked up heavy. I would say that I was holding on for my life. On the two bumps I caught air. On the second one, I thought, 'If I hit another one, I'm history.' There was no way I was going to be able to set my rail in and turn. I would just be skipping, skipping and then be stuck on the bottom, too low to pull in and too slow to out run it. I would have just gotten killed. So I was just holding on for my life and praying there wasn't going to be a third bump. I wasn't sure how much longer I could hold on.

Right at the takeoff, I made a decision to fade a little into the pocket, which was the difference between getting a bowl or not. Once I set my rail, it smoothed out when all the water got sucked up the face, like Pipeline. It smoothes itself out like tightening up a sheet. With my rail in there, I was able to start turning. I felt more at home. Then it set up perfectly, so I just pulled in. It looked insane! A slow motion, gigantic barrel! I could tell it was going to clam shell at the end by how the lip was tapering. I knew if I could hold on, I'd probably pop out the end, but I knew I had to hold on tight. So that's what I did. I held on tight and came out. What a rush!

169

7

9

11

170

To get that kind of feeling after you've been surfing so much in varied conditions, and heavy ones at that, I thought was really neat. It made me feel like a full grommet." — Mike Stewart

"I've walked down through Haleakala on through Kaupo Gap all the way to the ocean. It's just majestic! From moonscape to rain forest to desert." – Mike Stewart

Haleakalā

Kaupō Gap

View of West Maui, Lana'i and Moloka'i from Haleakalā

"Big wave sailing is what I wait for: it's the peak of the season. You only get the conditions five or six times a year. Sometimes you do it once a year, depends on the year. It's like the little fire in the back that's always waiting to go. It's the motivation that keeps you ready to go for it on those days. I don't think it ever gets boring. The level's always growing as to what's BIG. What's big is what's going to get me that feeling and Jaws definitely gets me that feeling. Sometimes I start thinking I could get killed in a car crash tomorrow driving home. Or I could have a heart aneurysm and die in my sleep. At least I'm having fun and this is really exciting. You want to be cautious and prepared, but if you're not enjoying it and ready to take whatever is coming, then you almost shouldn't be out there. Maybe I'm being stupid and I'm going to end up getting slapped by one, get knocked unconscious and become a coral head. But still, I'm not out there because of this challenge with fear. It's fun. I love it. If it's huge, there's definitely a certain amount of fear. But, by the same token, I know that if I spin out bottom turning, then I'm going swimming. You just got to stay calm. I should be ready to go down smiling, not panicking. If you get into that absolute worst possible place at big Jaws, you will be ripped into little pieces. You're not going to bounce around holding your breath. You will be pummeled, no question."

— Robby Naish

"It's funny that tow-in surfing came from
a group of windsurfers because our ultimate goal
with windsurfing was to get on a wave and just pitch
the sail. You wish your board could just turn into a little
surfboard. Now that's exactly what it's become."
– Mike Waltze

"*The whole reason I think every one of us started windsurfing, except Mike and the guys who originally started it, was when someone saw someone else do an aerial. That's what I saw. It looked fun and that's what all of this is about.*"
– Mark Angulo

1

2

*"Sometimes on my sailboard
I think, 'Man, I wish I was on
my surfboard because I could be
right where Laird is right now.'
With a sail in your hands, you have
the power of the wind and not as
much power of the wave. So we go
out to the bottom, then up to the top.
The surfers can stay right in the
pocket where all the power is."*
– Sierra Emory

Robby Seeger

Robby Naish

"We're dealing with a beast. People see the beauty and how we make it look easy, but Jaws is like a final exam." – Brian Keaulana

"On one of the bigger days we sailed, positioning was critical, so we were not riding waves together. On one wave, Robby Seeger was in front of Robby Naish. So Seeger pulls out the back only to find a much bigger wave behind it. The wind between the waves was only about eight knots, so Seeger pumped, but to no avail. He got to the top just as it started throwing. He tried to flick his equipment over the top and out the back as he dove through the lip. He made it through, but his equipment got sucked over the falls. His equipment looked like a toothpick as it went over the falls on a top to bottom barrel. Naish heroically sailed in and helped drag Robbie out of the impact zone. Seeger's equipment was destroyed." – Luke Hargreaves

Luke Hargreaves & Robby Seeger *191*

"A couple people have been horribly pounded by now. Luckily, no one has
drowned yet. But the heavy poundings of a few people have definitely shown the
rest of us that you've got to be careful and respect the place, respect the power it's
got and play it a little on the safe side." – Bjorn Dunkerbeck

"My biggest problem is, I got no plan. All of a sudden, it's like, should I turn now? You can't go into a wave telling yourself you're going to do a certain thing. You've got to just ride the wave. There's going to be a perfect situation and you're just going to do it. You can't plan. You've got to ride waves. Everyone's a different little beast. Just see what the wave offers you and pull it off if you can. They use to call me the Wet Noodle. I approach Pe'ahi totally different than I do other places. Sailing other spots, I'll try anything, anywhere. But out here, you're dealing with something different. Out here, you can die." – Mark Angulo

"It's a really cool perspective riding the same waves with the tow-in surfers. You can sit on the cliff or in the boat or even ride along on the ski, but it's totally different riding a wave with them. When I'm windsurfing with them, I'm right in the power pocket of the wave. You're riding and look up. There's Laird up in the top, cutting back right in the peak. Then you're at the top and Laird's way down there planting a bottom turn. It's really a rush to see, but it's all moving so fast that you could just as easy all hit each other." — Sierra Emory

"I've sailed it once or twice, but since towing it's been difficult because of the freedom towing has. I can go straight up wind, straight down wind, plus when you let go, you are unrestricted, making it possible to pull inside the barrel." – Laird Hamilton

"Surfers have a lot of catching up to do because the windsurfers are use to that speed and they already know how to judge the waves way out to sea." – Archie Kalepa

"*Freedom is a hard word to use sometimes because it's such an ordeal to get out there. It's work to do it, but what you get back from it is incredible. I know everyone who has sailed it. You see them and know instantly you have something in common. There's something there. It kind of makes everybody get along, in a sense.*" – Sierra Emory

Rush Randle

"Sailing it is different because the wave creates its own wind that comes straight up the face, plus the normal tradewinds that blow side off shore. Which is bad when you're behind a section because with the sail you are limited with your attack into the wind. With windsurfing, you've got to get into the wave way up wind, which is behind the peak. But once you're on it, you can go down the wave and do a little straight jaunt towards the peak and position yourself. It's fun!"
– Rush Randle

Paul Bryan & Laird Hamilton

4

207

"Jaws is always going to be separate because there's not a lot of people that can do it. Even some of the top names in windsurfing haven't pursued it. It's a different kind of thing. You really have to want it." – Sierra Emory

"It's just simply one nice perfect peak, just very tall. Simple windsurfing, come down from the peak, do a big bottom turn, then maybe one top turn, then go sail to the shoulder, then pull off. It's a perfect wave actually. Just real stoke, pure adrenalin."
– Hidemi Furuya

"The place, you've got to be kind of lucky to see it break. You've got to be even more lucky to get out there when it's breaking and you've got to be even luckier to even ride it. Just getting there and actually putting yourself in the spot and riding those mountains is a mission." – Bjorn Dunkerbeck

Josh Stone *213*

Pete Cabrinha

Robby Naish

Bjorn Dunkerbeck

Dave Kalama & Paul Bryan   215

"I caught that wave kind of deep from way outside. Mike was towing Laird into it also, so I thought maybe I shouldn't go. Everything was moving so fast and at that moment I was thinking, 'Should I bail or not because I have to drop down into it. If I pull out then there might be one right behind it and it's hard to waterstart right there and that's bad.' Then Mike and Laird bailed, so I changed my direction and went down wind. Then there was a big jump, then another big jump, so I couldn't set my rail. So when I got to the bottom, I finally caught my rail and looked up and the f#@king west peak was breaking already. It seemed like a five story building, then on top of that was a Greyline Hawaii bus. Then I decided, I couldn't make it. So I tried to go straight and run it out. I was out of power, so I jumped off. From the first part until then it was like five seconds, so fast. I got a good breath and tried to just cover my head and not panic. I touched the bottom, then I opened up my eyes and it was so dark and lots of pressure. Before that I didn't know which way to swim. So I kicked off the bottom and it was like fifteen strokes to the top. The most scary part was if I came up and there was a wave breaking. So there wasn't a wave right then and I was able to get two breaths before the next twenty feet of white water hit me. The first wave, I got deep. The second, I got distance. After that second one, I got more breaths. Then I saw Rush, but the rip pulled me down before he could get me.

I popped up again, but this time I drank so much water, I was choking. Then all of the sudden, Laird was right there with me in the water and he helped me get on Mike's ski. I almost blacked out. I can't imagine what would have happened to me if I wouldn't have touched the bottom or couldn't have gotten any breaths or there were no jet skis or friendship, friendship, most important. I really felt that after I saw the pictures. Then I knew that Laird jumped in. So many guys came and I really appreciated it. Myself, I don't want to die, but even more, I wouldn't want that to ruin it for them. Jaws, you cannot go alone by yourself, you need a team. Friendship, all good guys, good power, good vibrations, concentration, everything. Now I understand. When you wipe out anywhere else, it's not that serious, but out there it is. It's not their job. They are not there for rescue. It's very risky for them. You can lose a ski in the white water very easy. I think I spent probably 95% of my luck for my lifetime." – *Hidemi Furuya*

2

5

Hidemi Furuya *219*

"It's indescribable the rush and the whole adrenalin thing. When you're done, you feel like you conquered something so big and so insane. There's nothing like it for sure."
– Sierra Emory

Keith Teboul

Josh Stone

"When you go out there, everything, your whole life, gets put into perspective real quick." – Mark Angulo

Mark Angulo

Robby Naish

224   Greg Aguera

"That speed, adrenalin, power, the whole thing is just totally addicting. All these guys are just big kids. I feel the same in my head now as I did when I was a little kid and I'm sure they all feel the same way."
– Robby Naish

Roaming through page after page of surreal images, we easily forget the perilous nature of Jaws, and that these men are some of the world's best athletes, prepared to take on the extreme conditions. Through their varied activities in and around the ocean they've developed a respect for and an understanding of her many moods. They know they will not survive at Jaws without each other's help and caring. By teaming up and doing whatever is necessary to help one another be successful, they also reach a higher level of enjoyment and personal satisfaction.The genuine beauty of Maui is both powerfully dangerous and quietly vulnerable. It is rich with sensual stimulation, providing us with natural rollercoasters and an opportunity to live for the moment. If we observe and flow with Maui's unique spirit, we will find enjoyment in a place of unsurpassed potential and be inspired to preserve it for our children.